Errings

**POETS
OUT LOUD**

Elisabeth Frost, *series editor*

Errings

Peter Streckfus

Fordham
University Press
New York
2014

Copyright © 2014 Fordham University Press

All rights reserved. No part of this publication may be reproduced, stored in a retrieval system, or transmitted in any form or by any means—electronic, mechanical, photocopy, recording, or any other—except for brief quotations in printed reviews, without the prior permission of the publisher.

Fordham University Press has no responsibility for the persistence or accuracy of URLs for external or third-party Internet websites referred to in this publication and does not guarantee that any content on such websites is, or will remain, accurate or appropriate.

Fordham University Press also publishes its books in a variety of electronic formats. Some content that appears in print may not be available in electronic books.

Library of Congress Control Number: 2013955369

ISBN 978 0 823 25776 8

16 15 14   5 4 3 2 1

First edition

Contents

1

Heather Green 3
Videos of Fish 4
Patrimony 13
Erring 15

2

New Rules of the Ōan Era (1372) 41
Suggestions for a New Day (1452) 42
Additional New Rules, Suggestions for a New Day,
 & Cetera (1502) 43
Una Narrazione 44
Two Images of Oblivion 45
A Bridge, the Pilgrims 46
A Bridge, Election 52

3

The Reader 59
Bildungsroman 60
Time Ghazal 62
Earth and Water 64
The Lake and the Skiff 66
Transmigration 68

NOTES 77
ACKNOWLEDGMENTS 79

THERE CAME A CLOUD IT SETTLED ON YOUR SHOULDER.
    To soar through domes, bird of Art,
    Halfway to icy heaven.
—Barbara Guest

Every deep reader is an Idiot Questioner. He asks, "Who wrote my poem?"
—Harold Bloom

1

Heather Green

We were speaking of marsupial evolution.

Your head turned slightly away, you studied the touch screen.

It rained outside—drops struck the window, and, inches beyond, the berries of the beautybush shook under the rain.

I could not hear the rain striking the leaves, but I could hear the rain—you looked up from the screen to the window, and we viewed the rain together.

Light through the screen of rain brushed your ear, the folds and bridges of our love.

Summer rain.

In Benigni's film, you dream your love marsupial.

Why evolution, our text, the clock, and its placements.

From the light's lips to your ear—brief scrim of hair that coats the skin of ear.

Pocket into which I trust this my soul, shaking in the rain—

Pocket of silk, aquiver—

All poems are about time.

Videos of Fish

Body of Water

My mother is a fish declares Faulkner's youngest

in the novel that finds its points of view on the pathway

to Hades. All things, at their base, are water,

Thales, the first Western philosopher, tells me.

In life, my author, you chose birds to speak to,

whistling at them through the threshold of your door

from your wheelchair. I make now this poem, luminous,

hollow channels, to give you a place to occupy—

I give you water now, of which all things in this work

are composed. Be now a fish in this sky mirror,

soul body of the vertebrate animal,

chordata—head of light holes and life hole,

notochord, tail. As you lay dying,

I gave you this—drops for your tongue,

subtle rider of words, mute body of words:

here, a plastic straw to carry water to your lips.

Body of Moving and Light

Like a silvery fish pulled out of the dark water.

And so the opportunity for confusion

or clarity is intensified seven times.

The camera shakes, disorienting—

attached clandestinely to a belt,

hidden below a backpack worn front-wise,

it enters the market through an aisle between

two ice-covered, shallow cases that hold numerous fish,

some still moving—a cod head, disembodied,

opens its life hole repeatedly, as if

respiring, occupying the transitional state

between tank life and the next, the state of ice,

and then the interior of the fish market,

beyond the ice trays, tanks filled with separate species,

each tank large enough to hold a full-grown person inside.

Body of Dreams

Last night, my father came to my dreaming

self in the form of a vampire.

A vampire's position is liminal—

neither alive nor dead, both and neither,

nini-funi in Japanese, two-but-not-two.

The vampire, my father, no longer on this earth,

was on the earth but could not touch me

without hurting me, nor could he speak to the dead.

Unable to pass, he craved and feared his lasting.

A bardo is a boundary between states,

Tibetan in origin—a gap that can serve as a bridge,

an open span filled with an atmosphere of suspension,

neither this nor that, *nini-funi*. In Dante's

version, one is offered a definite end—

suffer for your mistakes, and you will ascend.

The bardo of self-cognizant wakefulness,

the bardo of dreams, the bardo of meditation,

the bardo that occurs at the moment of death,

the bardo of the luminosity of true nature,

the bardo of transmigration or true becoming—

where there is the death of one state of mind

there is the birth of another, and between these

there is bardo, it is said—he came to me like this—

he did not sleep like an animal, nor was he awake.

The ghost state, the purgatorial state, the dream state

—the fish circuiting their tanks. The Chinese of the vendors

in the background, the music in the market,

the white noise of water aerators. I hear the sounds

and feel a swimming sensation in my chest, a video

fiction, a trick I play on myself—orange, silver-gray,

and white ghost bodies—on each body that, fanlike,

tails the head, fanlike appendages—carp, perhaps thirty,

roiling around—one extends its jaws before its face

as a human person might lick the inside of his lips.

My dream ends with my father like a batman hero

swan diving off the roof of the building

on which we speak—incapable of flight, choosing pain

in place of death that would not yet come. I saw him jump

but didn't hear the sound of his body hitting the earth.

Body of Fish

Come to the surface of the screen with your light

and oxygen holes and press them for moments

against the page—as if seeking to pass through it.

Make with the trunk of your body the third letter—

in a motion move the ends of your face and caudal fin

each to the right, toward each other—C.

Toward the third hour on your axis—

and in the same motion sweep your trunk back,

tail beat pushing through the ninth hour, moving you then

headfirst in the new direction and off the screen—

this movement follow with movement of more bodies,

simultaneous, unselfconscious, aggregate—

choral, co-created, a gathering

of you in the mind—oscillate behind the screen like a wheel

of bodies, a promenade—it we you he she—

move through the water column, skins of bodies,

similar, discrete—company, crowd, collection,

shoal and plural movement of consciousness.

Setting and set by the turbid water in motion,

the new law of movement. Dissolution

and coming into being. Appear as lights

and images on the screen, your voices faded

to an inaudible and drawn-out *O!*

meaning *here is the place we asked for!*

Patrimony

Shadows from branches stirring—the evening sun shoots sharply through the leaves and window forming hundreds of camera obscuras, projecting, like a super-eight reel, on the wall.

The shadowed world.

Shadowing forth.

When I declared myself a poet, you handed me the pages of your book to finish and make public.

Shadows of bodies on bodies in a tank, all their erstwhile privations and wonderings.

Like souls, arms removed, replaced by silver fans, legs with plastic fins.

Rabbits and wolves and birds.

My only memory of you running, I am learning hide and seek.

A dash between the wooden bench you made for us and the banana tree in the corner of the yard, we run beside each other.

In the allegory of the cave the physical world is formed of shadow and echo.

Shadow figure: a man's mouth and brow, indicating fright.

Grizzled, painting your epic in naïve images on cardboard.

Dinner, cabbage and rice.

Peaches for dessert, Inka—dominoes, counting fives, and the card game gin.

On Thursdays, we'd watch Reitz's *Heimat*.

Come now, let us descend and hold converse with them.

Two bodies, two signs, for one voice.

Plato argues such a voice, because it exists as two, unchanging, is a dead voice.

Erring

As a boy winds the box of his music, opens the screen of his music, knowing the song to come,

You know, water, the song to come.

You placed it in me.

I, not in my senses, resembling a fountain, will tell you.

You were my age, devoted to the Virgin Mary and living in the mountains of Peru inland from Lima.

Desiring to leave behind the religious life, you wrote of a young boy taken by pirates.

The deck had a tumble-home effect with the center

of the boat as home—

the deck had a tumble-home effect with the center of the boat as home. On both sides were two double handled pumps (to empty the seepage) in

After the evening chow, Tuerto told me to retire early, so as to be lively on the morrow. I was to start as assistant cook. So I tailed the captain and his daughter to their cabin. He had sumptuous lodgings in the quarter deck. The captain began to read some yellow manuscripts while Dolores began to knit. She said that she was making a jerkin for her "novio." I sat down beside the glass-enclosed candle and began to make shadow play on the walls. I'd made the dog-and-cat-fight, the elephant procession, and was starting the duel of honor when I found Dolores standing behind me laughing, Te je, te je. "Edmundo, you clever with the ghost-play."

She glided over and knelt beside me.

"Well, get up nevertheless. I will dictate your prayers.

I will dictate your prayers.

Now, my dear, you see what we mean.

A golden life.

To find this lost thing, to find loss.

Also, *submission to me.*

Also, *taking.*

As in—

What pains it took me to dry your blue and lumpy skin, amor de Dios.

As in—

I was lost in the waves.

Until one in the foresheets with a pole-and-hook salvaged me and wrapped me close inside his coat, about his neck a metal drinking cup.

His warmth composed me so.

There were complaints from the hull and cargo at the slapping blows of the monster.

There was creaking, scraping, singing, groaning, clipping, and all decrescendoing into a splintering, ticking, and mousey noise.

Then there would follow the hurt sounds of whimpering, meowing, and cheeping, as the ship righted itself again.

Mounted before me you pointed to the sea village as we came to the lee of the island.

In the crimson light of human life—

Made fast to the shore, a dhow waited.

Its lateen sheet rattled in the wind.

This is how we learn.

Everything appears as light and images.

Rainbow bodies and bodies of darkness and water.

The Lamp of the White and Smooth Channel.

The far-reaching Water Lamp, and the Lamp of Space.

Dissolution and coming into being—

Later they began to occupy themselves with reading, feeding the fowls, and smothering the charcoal embers.

A flying fish skidded, staring wide-eyed, along the deck.

I recognized it from the one you had been wearing.

As we approached the polar waters, the days grew cold and squallish, and all hands were bunking below. The pilot had made me sleep topsides because of the crowded quarters. I chose to bunk in the topmost gig. It should have been roomy, twelve feet of keel, but inside were fish boxes, ledges, rigs, thwarts, and anchor gear, not to count the sail rigging and water lockers. Finally, with the parrot for company, I settled for the night between the fish box and the first thwart in the foresheets. I pulled the canvas a bit free away from the prow for ventilation.

Labyrinth filled with fiords, bays, inlets, forks, and a twisting.

Silver monsters the size of a donkey, they could not fly and used grass shrimp for bait.

With torches they lighted brush piles, and they simply kept the fire going night and day on the hilltops where they lived.

As all the others remained at the edge of the flock where the weak and the young were, three individuals ran up the hill.

They fell on our necks and cried—they were the maroons, shades, and had given up hope of ever seeing the living again.

Where is my father?

He is there close to the lips with the forefinger and thumb.

Which means *to speak*.

As we approached the polar regions, the days grew cold and

between the fishbox and the first thwart in the foresheets. I pull

— the gale.

During all this I somehow managed to hang on,

trough and nose into about 100,000 tons of water in the form of a wall.

So I got up and like a drunk and picked my way to the forecastle. Lucho with legs spread and holding on to the binnacle cowling was staring out into the sea. He was wrapped in his oilskin jersey. At first he said nothing to my greeting because he was so intent in keeping the galleon on her course. I just braced myself and stooped silently by and watched the whitecaps. They were all about like a procession of ghosts. Yet there was no moon to illuminate them. Still they seemed to give off light of themselves. Finally, Lucho reached over and put his hand on my shoulder saying, "Ola grumete. What do you think of this sea?"

Slowly blown ahead of the wind the pilot tied himself to the foremast.

He wanted to search for the corpses of the drowned.

By dawn most of them would be floating face down with crabs hanging on and disputing their bodies.

There was nothing.

Sea.

Not one saved himself.

I held myself, firstborn vulture from heaven.

A few seconds later I heard a voice in my ear.

I felt my language torn from my mouth, writhing on the deck like an eel out of water.

You shall be my page—

Your duty will be to stay always by my side and carry my musket and cutlass.

Reeds tied to a huge stone obtained by barter from the mountain people who sent their merchants.

My son, carry it around in your work.

We looked down into the blue of the glacier.

And we shuddered at the saddle.

And we started down the other side.

Now we came steadily through the low cloud ceiling.

We looked down into the blue ice of the glacier and shuddered at the saddle and started down the other side.

The valley of the Urubamba Everywhere we passed signs of wild life and the answer as to why it was uninhabited remained a mystery.

Although the wooded valley abounded in game, still it was hard to come by, because we were ignorant of the habits of the strange animals.

There were rats as big as dogs. These rodents had to be hunted at night when they came down in droves to drink in the river. There were quail that were caught only by the fleet of foot. The birds were so gorged with grain that they flew only a few yards at a time. They could be chased until they fell panting with exhaustion. Then they could be picked up. But to get them one had to hide under bushes and avoid detection.

There were fish in the river could be caught by good swimmers.

Now then you know the whole story.

Proudly we sing this day.

Pour out mellow notes.

Pull, pull, compadre, so tear away from me.

Lift my heart to heights serene.

Painfully.

My head will never be the light airy member its parents meant, made and presented to me in gratitude.

You leaned forward and put the question with living breath right into my ear.

And there I will keep it.

Like the wife of Lot, the historian.

My position ever gazing astern.

They rode their steeds out into the swells.

But the horses refused to swim very far.

So after shouting curses and threats the armed men turned back.

One of them dismounted.

And helped the viewer onto his horse.

Then mounting in front of you they galloped.

Toward the open book, the open shore, the open horse.

Hush now, quiet. Listen.

2

New Rules of the Ōan Era (1372)

If one has linked *kogaru*, "to burn," to the word "incense," then one should not introduce "crimson leaves" in a subsequent third verse, but use a word such as "boat." This is because "boat" makes for a change in the meaning of *kogaru*. By the same token, if one has linked "village" to a verse containing the word "smoke," then one should not use "brush burning" or any other kind of "firewood" in the third verse. And the same holds for all other cases of this sort.

—NIJŌ YOSHIMOTO, *New Rules of the Ōan Era (1372)*

Suggestions for a New Day (1452)

If one has linked *kogaru*, "to burn," to the word "incense," then one should not introduce "crimson leaves" in a subsequent third verse, but use a word such as "boat." This is because "boat" makes for a change in the meaning of *kogaru*. By the same token, if one has linked "village" to a verse containing the word "smoke," then one should not use "brush burning" or any other kind of "firewood" in the third verse. And the same holds for all other cases of this sort. In modern times there are those who contend that one should not link the word *omokage*, "image," to a word such as "dream" and then follow with "blossom" or "the moon" in a third verse, supposedly because the latter represent such strong "images" themselves. There is no reason for such a restriction, however; in the past such progressions were not avoided.

—ICHIJŌ KANERA (grandson of Yoshimoto), *Suggestions for a New Day* (1452)

Additional New Rules, Suggestions for a New Day, & Cetera (1502)

If one has linked *kogaru*, "to burn," to the word "incense," then one should not introduce "crimson leaves" in a subsequent third verse, but use a word such as "boat." This is because "boat" makes for a change in the meaning of *kogaru*. By the same token, if one has linked "village" to a verse containing the word "smoke," then one should not use "brush burning" or any other kind of "firewood" in the third verse. And the same holds for all other cases of this sort. If one has linked "cloud" to "evening shower" then it will not do to use "lightning" or "thunder" in a third verse; likewise, it will not do to link "Mount Fuji" to "snow," and then use "icehouse" in the third verse. And the same holds for all other cases of this sort. In modern times there are those who contend that one should not link the word *omokage*, "image," to a word such as "dream" and then follow with "blossom" or "the moon" in a third verse, supposedly because the latter represent such strong "images" themselves. There is no reason for such a restriction, however; in the past such progressions were not avoided.

—SHŌHAKU, *Additional New Rules, Suggestions for a New Day, & Cetera* (1502)

Una Narrazione

A man and woman came into a car with money.
Standing in the other's shadow, one pined for the other.

They were in the midst of an animated discussion.
The ting and the oven, knead the cinnabar and refine the mercury,
the topics of white.

"Get into the car" and "goodbye old paint" brushed on a pillar.
The trees of the grove turned bone white.

One need not hesitate to use "black pine" near the word "tree."
One needn't hesitate to paint "pine" at the edge of the words
"pillar of black."

Standing in the other's shadow, one pined for the other.
The words "pillar of black pine," "door of black pine" should
be parted from the word "tree" by at least five lines—

As the former are used as lumber.
The water and plastic of their things, standing in their shadows.

Two Images of Oblivion

An underdeveloped plot with poor drainage

Evenings we take the wheelchair around the apartments

Each orbit a pause to view birds where the ponds have formed

A mated pair of tree ducks, otherwise grackles

The male's double-voiced water song, then a dance

Sometimes a night heron

Years ago housing projects filled the plot

Before that, shacks of the Baptist settlement

No running water, a bronze pump, a lion on top

Plot where memory has no prior referent

Shallow flood of nothing

Yet a place all the same, like heaven or earth

The close of a nightly bedtime story

It always ended at the bottom of a hill

One rolled so fast he turned into hot butter

In the forest, buttered toast for all

A Bridge, the Pilgrims

Reapportion the desert, Font
                of Water Muddy as Graphite, young author.
Spell across the valley floor. As you hold
                your pencil, as you transcribe your *cat*, a *cup*,

the *car*, a *carp*, the *cap*, testing in lead
                the margin of civilization—
the letters cee, jot, vee, ell, zed, a, tee, o,
              and en—as you hold your pencil, so

The Reader, Storyteller, Idiot,
              and The Witness held their vessels of light
as they wrote themselves into the tent camp.
              The wind erupted and their papers flew:

Into the young woods our papers flew. The two others, who were assigned us by our supervisor, chased after the papers; meanwhile, Reader raised her eyes in the darkness and sighed, "This is a hoax. If we ever find anybody they'll be asleep." We ignored her, although truthfully our pursuit appeared hopeless. The Witness, from what seemed deep feeling, made the following verse:

> No one for the census but the moon, a shopping cart, rain-eaten styrofoam.

Such was his poem. As the composition
            of a young person (very close to your age, in fact)
it was appropriate, don't you think?
                    Each of the four agreed that this was so.

                              And so:

Finding there no enumerable citizens we directed our lights into the trees, and, impatient, the Reader entered them, her flashlight aimed toward a bridge. We followed and finally arrived behind her, before the bridge on which the highway spanned a small stream: "This is not marked on the map," someone huffed. But Reader put her keen nose to the ground and sniffed. She opened her mouth as if to speak then stared.

Following her gaze into that space beneath the bridge, we saw in that darkness a globule of light.

> The cave, you see, was actually located behind
> a huge waterfall

quoted Idiot, from his favorite book,

> Undifferentiated, a flock of monkeys, cloudy
> Luminosity.

Or the Lohans and a Bridge, which, remember,
     Young Font, must be separated by more than one verse.
And here a number of similar things that should not appear
          together in the same sheet: a Cavern,

Barrier-Gate, Hermitage, or a hermit's House or Residence;
     "To Abandon the World" and "Hermit
of the Priestly Way" (since the latter is one
     who has abandoned the world). Or once as

Bridge, once in "Venerable Bridgeway,"
     once in the synonym "rope bridge," one time
in the name of a famous such place.

And let there be just one instance of "floating bridge,"
                whether as such or in phrases like "floating
bridge of dreams," the title of the last chapter
                              of *The Tale of Genji*,

which leaves the young Ukifune
                          and the conclusion of the tale
in uncertainty. In short, to swim
                              in the world of illusion.

Let such rooms and structures
                stand as if open to the air at different heights,
linked to each other by rickety bridges or notched planks.

A Bridge, Election

We were speaking of dear Storyteller
                    and Idiot's exchange as they crouched
at the mouth of the homeless man's bridge,
                    tally devices and census cards in hand.

"Hello! Under the bridge!" yelled dear Idiot,
        as on their hands and knees they approached the glow.
Truly, you see: an open bed-chamber
                    below the overpass, and its dank vestibule,

the highway's basement, while civilization
                    at dawn above is hushed to thrums and clicks:

The traffic above hushed, and the water's music echoed off the ceiling as we approached. The light grew in radiance: on a concrete slab, at the edge of the embankment, a strange bubble. And as we neared, crawling, calling all the time, "Hello in the camp," "Excuse us," and "Good morning," the globule's surface moved, until, finally, we sensed its source: a large plastic sheet, illuminated within. We four cast sideways glances and took this as our text. The poem says:

> A suburban retreat bounding the capital, hidden
> from white cat and black
>
> crow alike, a small gilt figure in hermit's hat and dress:
> Tri-Color Bag.

A note, young author, is in order here.
         The Past, Ancient, Old Age, Death, and Living
do not belong to the category
                 of lamentation; The World, Parent and Child,

Moss Robes, Dark Sleeves, Hermitage, Abandoned
         Soul, Grieved Soul, and Life, on the other hand,
mark a verse as a lamentation.
                 Separate by at least five verses words

associated with this category.
         And thus: white-haired, retired and half asleep,
holding a light (for rats), a cup, and a cover
                 of plastic, their subject sat up on his

concrete bed and allowed them to count him.

Westing, he had perceived a call, he testified, and headed into Arlington. We all nodded and scribbled furiously. In his bag: a rope of horse hair, a yarn of human hair, and a dog hair hat. And as we recorded, the sign was tendered: "Click," went the counting device in the hand of a team member who that morning had just joined us, and whom we have yet to introduce here, as until that instant we barely noticed him ourselves. But after we turned, looked, and eyed one another, we recognized in him the office—not grown up yet, in the form of a young man freckled as if God had spilled coffee grounds on him, an accident. "Thank you, Citizen," our newly elected said, deep under the bridge of George Washington Hwy at the corner of Kilgallen.

And so they found you, young author, behind them.
Draw a picture here of an alligator with a brimmed hat on, a skunk, possum, turtle, and you.

Then the hermit wiped his eye and returned to sleep.

Draw here the letter em, the letter e.

3

The Reader

Experience among the waves allows one to limit the field.

Each year he grew another soul, oblong, slightly pointed at the end, like an oar, its surface turned to the light.

Blacken now and lift your news into the air.

Bildungsroman

Where am I.

A window, blinds half opened, the maple and beautybush and smilax catching the lamplight, nodding as if a silent chorus. Beyond, the flood of the nothing audience.

How much easier it is to address you when I cannot see you, turned dark, in the blackness of the sure mistake.

In the dreams, disorder in a house is marked by water.

At the end of a hose, a meter—a white plastic waterwheel—is broken.
Pipes leak above a basement swimming pool.
Cracked and empty, a sheet metal tank, caked with lime.

Who could we be to you, we whom you never knew, your siblings—we who could not swim until adulthood.

At three and five years old, before I was born, my two older sisters were lost in the canal adjacent to the children's park, having found a way to open the back gate, and closing it.

We spoke to you, my siblings and I. We pretended.

Older than us, you told us how to behave among children at school, how to find friends, if only we could hear you.

How does one return to a story like yours without trying to stop it in the mind.

Its bricks and pillars.

The dream-spur on the heel of the dog that bit me, that turned its eye from the subject as if it were not the subject.

We were each a child among children, my siblings and I. They followed me. I was named the oldest.

Our father watched from the front porch in his lawn chair. My twelfth summer, he allowed us to ride bikes out of his sight.

Paths through fields. On the banks of a ditch, a shady clearing formed by trees, and in one, an abandoned tree house. Each day after riding the dusty trails on our street bikes, we rested there.

What did we do, brothers, sitting on the platforms joined by rickety plank bridges and ladders. Did we tell stories together. Strive, contend, and vote. Were we of one mind, pretending.

Who made the tree house and the trails we rode.

Other children who we never saw, we guessed. Children from the past. We thought about them as we rode and rested on their platforms, sharing a single soda between ourselves.

Time Ghazal

There is fire in the beginning—without it, we thought, we could not see one another.

After only months, a scorched foothill, but covered in evergreen heather.

We did not prefer it this way, love, cutting our feet on the stones of the hill as we ascended,

Scratching ourselves among the browns and greens of the heather.

On a sunny morning you fancied you might distinguish with the naked eye the deer that sometimes wandered from adjacent forests,

Or even the hares that began to swarm above the line of heather.

We simply found ourselves here, the ghosts of the grouse, deer, and hares all straying in the morning fog—

Under which we also strayed, the hillside violet in its fog blossom, can you see this, Heather.

You spoke—I listened in my silence, lost in and clinging to it, filled with fear and longing, thinking.

Thinking, come brush the stone of my tongue, grow beside it a flaming branch of heather.

On the northern face, we watched the noon sun light the fog just above the rise,

A small child on the hill, the interior of her heart like a gem, all over flowered with heather.

Earth and Water

Shape a small mouth, the size of a coin, on the other bank.

Around the mouth trace the features and body of a small person.

"Yes, this one has fruit," said another who looked above and discerned a fruit the color and texture of a lemon.

We then noticed in the branches more such fruit, elongated and yellow, shaped almost as if each held inside it a human form, some as full as grown persons.

It was important that we not rouse them as they slept.

In their waxed canvas and tweed, as if kings, they hunted highland fowl.

The spirits taught their dogs to gather discs.

Little canals running all over.

And we were constantly falling into them in the darkness and drowning.

All of this to produce a childhood.

You my young thing, you shaped like a mouse, like an ear.

A rosy blush on the lobe.

Be born by three right here.

The Lake and the Skiff

Tell me again about the lake of the poem.

The little skiff.

In which you were curled, like an infant in its bed.

The dark canopy of sky rattling above.

Standing at your bedside, we recounted our tale to you.

The regularity of our speech prevented the breezes being so discursive.

You looked out through your eyes at us and blinked to show you heard.

We said we'd little time before the city gates shut.

This revealed to you the error in the doctrine that maintains among the numerous souls within us one is more aflame.

As we paddled away, to speak and rest together, the wind took up its chorus.

Straightening your body, you said nothing.

Lord Marpa the translator said, "Sons, if you do phowa, do it like this," then a sphere of five-colored light the size of an egg ascended into the sky from a crack at the crown of his head.

Then we were left alone, like dwellings unconnected.

Search, confused one, around your shores if any parts of you rejoice in peace.

The flight path of a bird in the sky, the channel cut by a fish as it glides, the void of dreams. How difficult it is to remain one person.

Transmigration

You looked, my love, into your field glasses
                                    at a large shorebird,

               as over and over again it plunged its long bill
like a lance, upcurved
and darker at the end,
into the muck, to the hilt.

It spread the dawn-colored heaven of its wings and breast,
and then turned its back
               and showed the marbled dusk of its outer wing.

It seemed a film,
a silent television,

to which the white noises about you—whispered
         voice of your companion, breath, waves at your toes—
were a displaced, incongruous soundtrack.

You raised the lenses to your eyes again and you
            were near, its walk through the muck, its strange, long
                                    organ stitching

the mud, its kin beside it pecking the surface.

"How real a proximity that cannot be
accompanied by touch, how real the mud

'at a distance'?" you wrote,

having lost sight of it, as it flew

                      out over the lake of your own illusion.

Love, some of our movements could be explained by natural laws, but some cannot be. Sympathetic

associates and friends blamed the unexplained portion on the sun's warping of nearby space. Clocks move more

slowly in stronger gravitational fields, they said, and this you briefly took to heart. Later this month

you will join a space center assessing an Antarctic lake located miles beneath an ice sheet, a

kind of laboratory for the development of technologies to explore the suspected sub-surface of our unexplained distance.

You looked through the glass to the sky, broken
only by the panes

of the observatory, no more than
a solarium

in reality.
Some would call it a body. And the sky

said nothing. Sheer sky.
The clouds said even less, shaped like thoughts

instead of bodies. Dry God, where is the God
of Rain? Sleeping God

where are you? At home you found in the bird books an illustration titled "Godwit." The godwit, long, bicolored bill, its over-large eye. The image reminded you of figures in paintings by Bosch. Paintings of life are always a repetition of death and oblivion. And poetry?—you came back into bed beside me, yet asleep, and put your hand on my side—at sleep's length—at arm's length.

And there in bed were my empty shells, nested like a softball
in a bushel basket at the center of the District of Columbia:

a trinity of pronoun cases,
the three stooges, the father the son the holy book,

increasingly invisible specks suspended inside of me,
occupying no more than one billionth of the real volume of me.

Love. Love, couldn't you see?
No, you said. No. Tell me. Tell me.

Notes

The first epigraph, taken from the poem "Bird of Art," elides Guests's second line, "The cloud seeks high culture after Ovid." "Bird of Art" is the second poem in Guest's sequence "Miniatures." The second epigraph comes from *The Anxiety of Influence*.

"Erring" adapts language and typewritten pages from *Two Golden Earrings*, an unpublished manuscript by Robert Streckfus (1921–2009) c. 1957–59 and 1978–79, and is inspired by Guest's "Miniatures."

"New Rules of the Oan Era (1372)," "Suggestions for a New Day (1452)," "Additional New Rules, Suggestions for a New Day, & Cetera (1502)," "Una Narrazione," and "A Bridge" adapt language from Shōhaku's *Renga Rule Book of 1501* (translated by Steven D. Carter), a layered commentary written over the course of some 130 years in three voices by three authors. "A Bridge" also takes from *The Tosa Diary*, written by Ki no Tsurayuki (872–945), and is inspired by Sabrina Orah Mark's *The Babies*.

"The Lake and the Skiff," in its last sentence, repeats from Czeslaw Milosz's "Ars Poetica" (translation, Robert Hass).

Acknowledgments

Thank you to the editors of these journals in which poems from this collection, often in different versions, first found readers: *Chicago Review, Colorado Review, New Orleans Review, The New Republic, Pleiades, Poem-A-Day* (Academy of American Poets), *The Seattle Review, Sentence, Slate, West Branch,* and *The Volta.*

Deep gratitude to the Peter S. Reed Foundation and the University of Alabama Research Grants Committee for support; to Jennifer Browne, Jessica Fisher, Elisabeth Frost, Ilya Kaminsky, Dana Levin, James Longenbach, D. A. Powell, Spencer Reece, Carol Snow, Kathryn Starbuck, Linus Streckfus, Paul Streckfus, Susan Tichy, my University of Alabama students and colleagues, and, vitally, Louise Glück, for reading, conversation, and advice that made this possible; and to Heather, my guide and companion, in writing and love, along the way.

POETS OUT LOUD PRIZE WINNERS

Sara Michas-Martin
Gray Matter

Peter Streckfus
Errings
EDITOR'S PRIZE

Amy Sara Carroll
Fannie + Freddie: The Sentimentality of Post–9/11 Pornography

Nicolas Hundley
The Revolver in the Hive
EDITOR'S PRIZE

Julie Choffel
The Hello Delay

Michelle Naka Pierce
Continuous Frieze Bordering Red
EDITOR'S PRIZE

Leslie C. Chang
Things That No Longer Delight Me

Amy Catanzano
Multiversal

Darcie Dennigan
Corinna A-Maying the Apocalypse

Karin Gottshall
Crocus

Jean Gallagher
This Minute

Lee Robinson
Hearsay

Janet Kaplan
The Glazier's Country

Robert Thomas
Door to Door

Julie Sheehan
Thaw

Jennifer Clarvoe
Invisible Tender

www.ingramcontent.com/pod-product-compliance
Lightning Source LLC
Chambersburg PA
CBHW020701300426
44112CB00007B/473